**Christine Webster**

**Weigl**

Published by Weigl Educational Publishers Limited
6325 10th Street S.E.
Calgary, Alberta, Canada T2H 2Z9

Website: www.weigl.com


Library and Archives Canada Cataloguing in Publication
Webster, Christine
Salish / author: Christine Webster ; editor: Heather Kissock.
(Aboriginal peoples of Canada)
Includes index.
Also available in electronic format.
ISBN 978-1-55388-646-4 (bound).--ISBN 978-1-55388-652-5 (pbk.)
. Salish Indians--Juvenile literature. I. Kissock, Heather
II. Title. III. Series: Aboriginal peoples of Canada (Calgary, Alta.)
E99.S2W432 2010 j971.004'979435 C2009-907319-6

Printed in the United States of America in North Mankato, Minnesota
1 2 3 4 5 6 7 8 9 14 13 12 11 10

062010
WEP230610

Photograph and Text Credits
Cover: Canadian Museum of Civilization (VII-G-584, S97-18075); Alamy: pages 4, 8, 16T, 20; British Columbia Archives: pages 6 (AA-00264), 21T (I-51433); Canadian Heritage Gallery: page 12; Canadian Museum of Civilization: pages 9T (II-C-396, D2003-08785), 9M (II-C-344, D2003-08414), 9B (II-C-208 a-b, D2003-08529), 13B (VII-D-115, D2002-004800), 16B (VII-D-158, D2004-07196), 21B (II-E-18, S95-05958); CP Images: page 17; Getty Images: pages 5, 7, 10, 11, 13T, 14, 15, 22, 23.

Every reasonable effort has been made to trace ownership and to obtain permission to reprint copyright material. The publisher would be pleased to have any errors or omissions brought to their attention so that they may be corrected in subsequent printings.

All of the Internet URLs given in the book were valid at the time of publication. However, due to the dynamic nature of the Internet, some addresses may have changed, or sites may have ceased to exist since publication. While the author and publisher regret any inconvenience this may cause readers, no responsibility for any such changes can be accepted by either the author or the publisher.

We gratefully acknowledge the financial support of the Government of Canada through the Canada Book Fund for our publishing activities.

# The People

The Salish are a **First Nation**. They live in the southern part of British Columbia, including Vancouver Island. They are also found in parts of the northwestern United States.

Canada's Salish are made up of two groups. The Coast Salish live along the southern coast of the province. The Interior Salish live farther inland. Most Salish live on **reserves** in these areas. Some live in cities and towns.

## NET LINK

To learn about the history of the Salish people, go to **www.multiculturalcanada.ca/Encyclopedia/A-Z/a10/1**.

# Salish Homes

## LONGHOUSES

In the past, the Salish lived in large homes called longhouses. Longhouses were most often made with red cedar planks. Cedar was used because it was more waterproof than other trees in the area. It helped keep water out of the home.

## Salish Ideas

Longhouses were big enough to house several people. Entire families lived in them. These families included fathers, mothers, and children, as well as grandparents, aunts, uncles, and cousins.

Inside, the floors of the longhouse were made of earth. Mats often covered the bare ground. The walls were lined with low platforms for sleeping. Above the platforms were storage shelves. Several fire pits kept the house warm.

# Salish Clothing

## PONCHOS AND ROBES

On rainy days, the Salish wore cedar ponchos. Men wore cedar bark robes at special events.

In warm weather, Salish women wore aprons made from cedar bark. When it turned cold, they wore dresses.

## CAPES

The Coast Salish used the furs from small animals, such as beavers, rabbits, and squirrels, to make capes and other coverings.

## DECORATION

Salish clothing was often decorated with fur, porcupine quills, animal teeth, shells, or bear claws. Necklaces made of bear claws, shells, beaver teeth, and snakeskin were used as jewellery.

## BREECHCLOTHS

Salish men sometimes wore breechcloths made from animal skin. These were small flaps of fabric that looked like underwear. If the weather was cold, the Salish would wear shirts and leggings.

# Hunting and Gathering

## SALMON

Salmon was a main food for the Salish. Once caught, some salmon was eaten immediately. The rest was dried for use in winter.

## CLAMS

Women were responsible for digging clams from the beach. The clams were removed from their shells and smoked.

## WHALE

Whales provided the Salish with oil. Whale oil was rubbed onto canoes to **preserve** them. It was also used to store berries.

The Salish relied on food sources found nearby in nature. The ocean supplied the Coast Salish with much of their food. Deer and other small animals were hunted by both the Coast and Interior Salish. Berries and roots were also found throughout their territories.

## SOAPBERRIES

Soapberries were a common treat. The Salish used them to make sweets such as ice cream and beverages.

## DEER

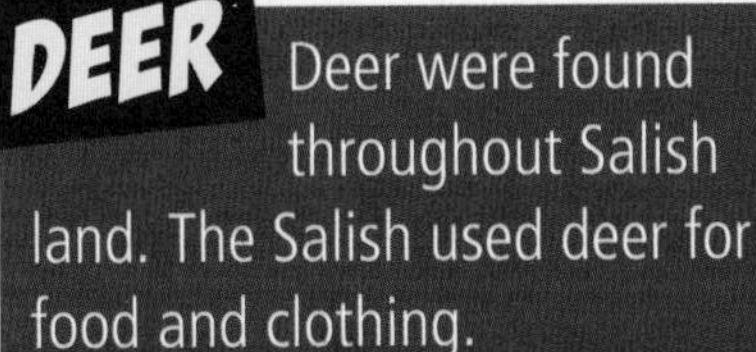

Deer were found throughout Salish land. The Salish used deer for food and clothing.

## ROOTS

The Salish gathered roots, such as turnips and parsnips, in summer. The roots could be dried or baked before eating.

# Salish Tools

## WEIRS

The Salish used **weirs** to catch fish. These fencelike structures blocked fish from swimming up or down the river. The fish became crowded in one area. This made it easy for the Salish to spear a large number of fish at a time.

## Salish Ideas

Salish knives were made from sharpened seashells. Wet sand was used like sandpaper to smooth the blades. The blades were then tied to wooden handles with bark **twine**.

## DIGGING STICKS

Digging sticks were made from hard wood. They were sharpened to a point. Then, a horn or antler was added to the end. These sticks were used to dig up dirt when planting seeds or to dig up clams to eat.

# Moving from Place to Place

## CANOES

The Coast Salish used canoes for fishing and visiting other villages. Salish canoes could be up to 18 metres long and carry more than 40 people.

When building a canoe, the Salish used fire to bring down the tree. They lit the fire at the tree's base and let it burn right through the tree. The tree then fell.

## NET LINK

See the steps involved in building a Coast Salish canoe at **www.virtualmuseum.ca/Exhibitions/Traditions/English/salish_canoe_06.html**.

# Salish Music and Dance

Drumming was an important part of Salish music. The Salish used both handheld drums and box drums. Box drums were often made from cedar. Sometimes, they had paintings on them.

The Salish used drums in many ways. People listened to them, danced to them, told stories with them, and sang along with them.

## NET LINK

Read about the Salish Spirit Dance at **www.multiculturalcanada.ca/Encyclopedia/A-Z/a10/5**.

# The Raven

Long ago, Grey Eagle was the guardian of water, fire, the Sun, the Moon, and the stars. He did not share these objects with the people on Earth, however, because he did not like them. Instead, he hid them from view.

One day, a beautiful white bird called Raven came to visit Grey Eagle. He noticed the items that Grey Eagle was hiding. Raven felt he had to take them and put them to use so that the world would be a better place to live. He quickly hung the Sun in the sky, and when it set, he put the Moon and the stars up in the sky. As the Moon shone down on him, he dropped the water to the Earth, where it spread to become rivers, lakes, and oceans. All that was left to set up was fire.

Raven put the fire in his beak and started to fly, but the smoke blew back over him, turning his feathers black. The heat caused him to drop the fire. It landed on two rocks, which is why, to this day, rubbing two rocks together will produce fire.

As for Raven, he was never able to remove the smoke from his feathers. He remained black for the rest of his days.

# Salish Art

The Salish were known for their excellent carving. They were especially known for the large **totem poles** they carved from huge cedar logs. The totem poles usually featured humans, birds, and other animals.

Coast Salish women were skilled in weaving baskets from cedar. They used the bark and the roots of cedar trees to make the baskets.

## NET LINK

To learn about another type of Salish weaving, go to **www.coastsalishweaving.com/history.html**.

## Make Soapberry Ice Cream

### Ingredients

1 cup soapberries
1/4 cup water
Sugar

### Equipment

Bowl
Spoon or potato masher

### Directions

1. Place the berries in a bowl.
2. Add the water to the berries.
3. Add a dash of sugar on top for sweetness.
4. Mash the berries, water, and sugar together until the mixture foams into a pink froth.
5. Enjoy your soapberry ice cream.

# Glossary

**First Nation:** a member of Canada's Aboriginal community who is not Inuit or Métis

**preserve:** to prepare food for future use

**reserves:** areas of land set aside for First Nations to use

**totem poles:** large, upright poles that are carved and painted with First Nations emblems

**twine:** strong string

**weirs:** fences placed across streams to catch fish

# Index